BUTTERFLIES FOR KIDS

BUTTERFLIES FOR KIDS

A JUNIOR SCIENTIST'S GUIDE to the Butterfly Life Cycle and Beautiful Species to Discover

JUNIOR SCIENTISTS

LAUREN DAVIDSON

ROCKRIDGE PRESS

Interior and Cover Designer: John Calmeyer
Art Producer: Samantha Ulban
Editor: Annie Choi
Production Editor: Ruth Sakata Corley

ISBN: Print 978-1-64739-884-2 | eBook 978-1-64739-578-0
R1

Printed in China

CONTENTS

CONTINUED →

BUTTERFLIES UP CLOSE (CONTINUED)

WELCOME, JUNIOR SCIENTIST!

Have you ever watched butterflies and wanted to know more about them? Perhaps you've wondered if they sleep at night. Why do some butterflies have colorful wings but others look plainer? And how exactly do chubby caterpillars transform into beautiful, graceful butterflies? If you have thought about these things, you are a junior scientist!

In this book, you will learn about these fascinating insects. You will discover how caterpillars grow, what happens inside a chrysalis, and how butterflies find mates. You will explore unusual butterfly behaviors like basking and puddling. Finally, you will get up close and personal with some of the most amazing butterfly species you may see in your own backyard.

Do you have a butterfly growing kit? Great! This book will also show you what to look for as your caterpillars grow and turn into butterflies.

PART ONE

AMAZING BUTTERFLIES

With their bright colors and pretty wings, butterflies are well loved. Did you know there are more than 17,000 known butterfly **species** on Earth? Each has its own **adaptations**, or ways of surviving in its habitat. Scientists think there are still thousands of species waiting to be discovered.

Butterflies can be found all over the world except Antarctica. This is because they have **evolved** over millions of year to live in many environments. But you don't have to travel far to find butterflies; you can easily find them in parks, forests, and even your own backyard!

Depending on where you live in North America, you can probably find 100 or more species near your home. Grab a notebook and pencil and ask if you can go outside. If you find a butterfly, take notes and sketch it in your book. Someday you might even be a **lepidopterist**, or butterfly scientist!

The Arctic butterfly can survive in freezing temperatures.

What Is a Butterfly?

Butterflies are **insects**. Insects are **invertebrates** with no bones and a tough outer shell called an exoskeleton. The exoskeleton is made of chitin, which is like the material that forms your fingernails! Like all invertebrates, butterflies are cold-blooded, which means they must absorb heat from their environment.

Like most insects, butterflies have three body parts—head, thorax, and abdomen—two antennae, six legs, and four wings. But they have differences that make them stand out from other insects. For example, their wings are covered in scales made of the same material as their exoskeleton, and butterflies taste with their feet.

Can you name other insects you know? How are they different from butterflies? How are they similar?

Ancient Butterflies

Before butterflies, there were moths. Moths first appeared about 100 million years ago. These ancient moths had to adapt to changing weather, food in short supply, and plants that were still evolving. Scientists believe these adaptations are what made butterflies evolve from these insects.

The oldest butterfly fossil is 40 to 50 million years old. Ancient butterflies looked a lot like today's butterflies but were probably less colorful.

***Prodryas persephone*, an extinct butterfly found in a fossil from Eocene rocks**

Meet the Insect Class

Plants and animals are divided into groups and named through a method called taxonomy. It might help you to think of taxonomy as a ladder. The top rung stands for all life-forms on Earth. With each step down, we get more information about the life-form's description.

Every living thing on Earth can be described using the eight rungs of the taxonomy ladder: domain, kingdom, phylum, class, order, family, genus, and, finally, species. Butterflies belong to the order of insects called Lepidoptera. The chart on the opposite page shows the taxonomy of *Danaus plexippus*. You probably know this insect by its common name: the monarch butterfly.

DID YOU KNOW?
The word *Lepidoptera* means "scaly wings."

DOMAIN	EUKARYA	**ALL ANIMALS AND PLANTS**—about 2,000,000 known species
KINGDOM	ANIMALIA	**ALL ANIMALS**—about 1,260,000 known species
PHYLUM	ARTHROPODA	**ALL INVERTEBRATES WITH AN EXOSKELETON**—about 1,200,000 known species
CLASS	INSECTA	**ALL INSECTS**—about 1,000,000 known species
ORDER	LEPIDOPTERA	**ALL BUTTERFLIES AND MOTHS**—220,000 known species
FAMILY	NYMPHALIDAE	**ALL BRUSH-FOOTED BUTTERFLIES**—6,000 known species
SUBFAMILY	DANAINAE	**MILKWEED BUTTERFLIES**—300 known species
GENUS	*DANAUS*	**TIGER MILKWEED BUTTERFLIES**—12 known species
SPECIES	*PLEXIPPUS*	**MONARCH BUTTERFLY**—1 species

From Antennae to Hindwing

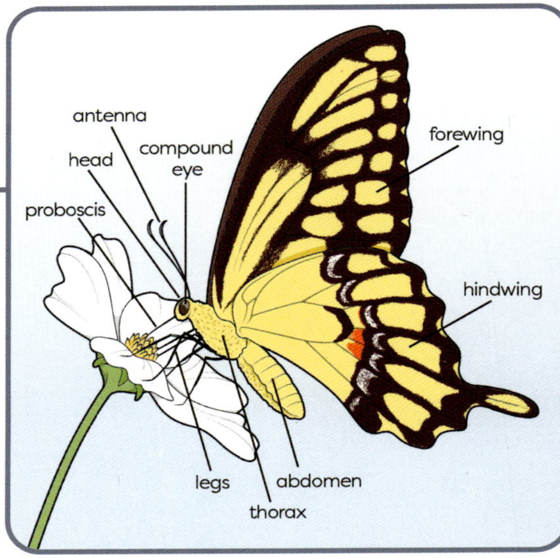

Butterflies come in all shapes and sizes. One of the smallest species, the western pygmy blue, has a **wingspan** of only ½ inch—about as wide as a dime. But the endangered Queen Alexandra's birdwing can have a wingspan of more than 10 inches!

Like all insects, butterflies have six legs and three body parts: head, thorax, and abdomen. The head has two eyes and two antennae. Butterflies see colors better than many insects. They use their antennae for smelling. Butterflies have a long, straw-like mouth called a proboscis. Four wings are attached to the thorax. Speaking of wings, they get their shape from tubelike structures called wing veins and are covered in tiny scales. Butterflies breathe through small holes called spiracles that are located on the sides of their abdomens.

DID YOU KNOW?

Some butterflies, like the zebra longwing, have an unusual way of mating. The adult male may mate with the female before she has even fully emerged from her chrysalis!

Butterfly or Moth?

Although it's sometimes tricky, you can tell butterflies and moths apart. Butterflies are usually brightly colored and active during the day. Moths are generally less colorful and active at night. Moth wings often blend in with their surroundings, which lets them camouflage while resting during the day. Butterflies have threadlike antennae with knobs at the ends. Moths tend to have feathery antennae. Butterflies are often slim, whereas moths often have thick, fluffy bodies to keep in body heat while flying at night. But there are exceptions to all these rules!

BUTTERFLY	MOTH
Bright, colorful wings	Dull-looking wings
Thin and smooth body	Thick and fuzzy body
Threadlike, clubbed antennae	Feathery or straight antennae
Closed wings at rest	Open wings at rest
Active during the day	Active at night

A Butterfly's Life

Butterflies have four life stages: egg, **larva**, **pupa**, and adult. The butterfly begins life as an egg. After a week or so, a tiny larva, or caterpillar, hatches. The caterpillar's purpose is to eat and grow as much as possible. After weeks of growing, it finds a safe place and becomes a **chrysalis**. Inside this pupa, the caterpillar changes into an adult butterfly. This can take several days or sometimes much longer. When conditions are right, the adult butterfly comes out.

This life cycle is called complete **metamorphosis**. Many insects—like bees, flies, beetles, and even fleas—have the same life cycle. Other insects, like grasshoppers and cockroaches, have an incomplete metamorphosis with three stages: egg, nymph, and adult. These insects look mostly the same throughout their lives, except adults often have wings.

A CLOSER LOOK

Each butterfly species has a way to survive the winter. This is called **overwintering**. Some butterflies **migrate** to warmer places. Others go into a resting period where they don't eat or develop further until it is warm again. Depending on the species, they may overwinter as eggs, pupae, caterpillars, or even as adult butterflies.

A Tiny Beginning

Each butterfly species lays its eggs on a specific type of plant. This is its **host plant**. Egg-laying usually happens in the warmer months of spring through fall. Butterflies find the perfect plant by tasting with their feet as they land. Once a butterfly mom finds a host plant, she usually lays her eggs on the undersides of the leaves.

Eggs can be smooth and perfectly round, patterned and oval, or any shape in between. They can be laid one at a time or in groups. It's not easy to be an egg. Weather changes and predators are very real dangers. Most eggs hatch in about a week, but some **hibernate** for months through winter. A butterfly lays several hundred eggs in her life-time to make sure enough survive.

DID YOU KNOW?
Because of predators, diseases, and other factors, more than 90 percent of butterfly eggs don't make it to adulthood.

The Hungry Caterpillar

When the time is right, tiny larvae chew their way out of the eggs. At this point, the caterpillars aren't much bigger than the eggs themselves. This second stage of the life cycle is all about growing. Many caterpillars eat their eggshell as a first meal. It gives them nutrients to begin their tiny journeys. Then they start feeding on their host plant. Sometimes they munch their plant until there is nothing left. After a few weeks of feeding, a caterpillar can be more than 1,000 times the size it was when it hatched!

BUILT TO EAT

A caterpillar has six legs on its thorax that it uses for walking, but its long body needs extra help holding on. Soft, leglike parts on its abdomen, called prolegs, provide help. Hook-like grippers on the tips of the prolegs help it grip onto surfaces.

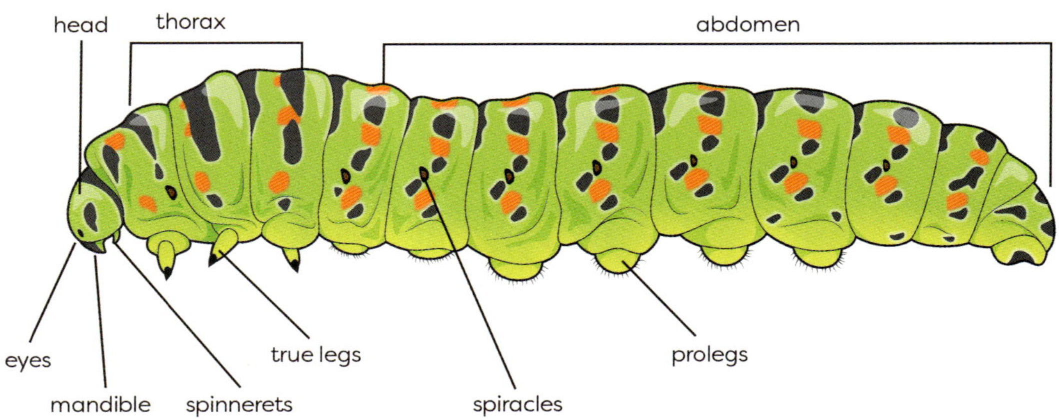

The caterpillar has several pairs of eyes, but it can't see very well. It uses its tiny antennae to smell around to find food. Strong, chewing mouthparts, called mandibles, allow the caterpillar to constantly munch its host plants. Some caterpillars look smooth, and others are spiky or fluffy and covered in hairs.

FINDING FOOD

Most caterpillars eat only their host plant during this stage. To get the nutrients they need, caterpillars must eat a lot. They feed constantly—for anywhere from several days to several weeks. Because caterpillars eat so much, they make a lot of frass, or poop.

Some caterpillars also eat other creatures. One caterpillar, known as the large blue, can copy ants' communication signals. The ants are tricked into thinking the caterpillar is an ant, and they take the caterpillar to their colony. Once inside the nest, the butterfly larva feeds on the ants' eggs and larvae!

DID YOU KNOW?
No one knows where the word *butterfly* came from, but people think it may have been used to name yellow, or butter-colored, butterflies.

I'M MOLTING!

Exoskeletons can't stretch, so insects must shed them to grow bigger. When a caterpillar needs more room to grow, its exoskeleton splits near its head. The larva crawls out of the opening and reveals a new larger skin that formed underneath. This process is called **molting**.

Most species go through five **instars**, or the stages between each molt. The first instar is when the caterpillar hatches. The second instar starts after its first molt, and so on. Caterpillars can't grow without molting, and it's very dangerous. Their new skin is soft, so they must stay very still while it hardens. Because they aren't moving, it's much easier for predators to catch them. Once the new skin hardens, many caterpillars eat their old skins!

Monarch caterpillars molting

Snapshots of the molting process (in order from top to bottom)

Pupa Prep

During its last instar, the caterpillar wanders away from its host plant. It looks for a safe, protected place like a leafy bush. To prepare for its final molt, the caterpillar uses its mouth to weave a silk pad. It then hooks its abdomen to the silk and begins to curl its body. Its exoskeleton splits open like all its other molts. But this time, the larva doesn't crawl out of it. It wiggles around instead. This movement helps bunch up the old skin to reveal the fully formed chrysalis. Once the chrysalis hardens, the pupal stage can last anywhere from a few days to a couple of years.

DID YOU KNOW?
When a butterfly emerges from its chrysalis, its proboscis is in two parts. One of the first things it must do is zip it up!

A monarch butterfly chrysalis hanging from a branch

A CLOSER LOOK

Chrysalis means "gold" in Greek. Many butterfly pupae have small golden dots or look like they are made of metal. During this phase, special proteins called enzymes melt away the larva's shape. At the same time, the butterfly's features begin to form. If you look closely at a chrysalis, you can see parts of the wings, antennae, legs, and proboscis.

Cocoon and chrysalis are both insect pupa stages, but the word *chrysalis* is unique to butterflies. A cocoon is the silk pouch that some moth caterpillars spin around their pupae. Other types of insect larvae, like several wasps and flies, also make cocoons.

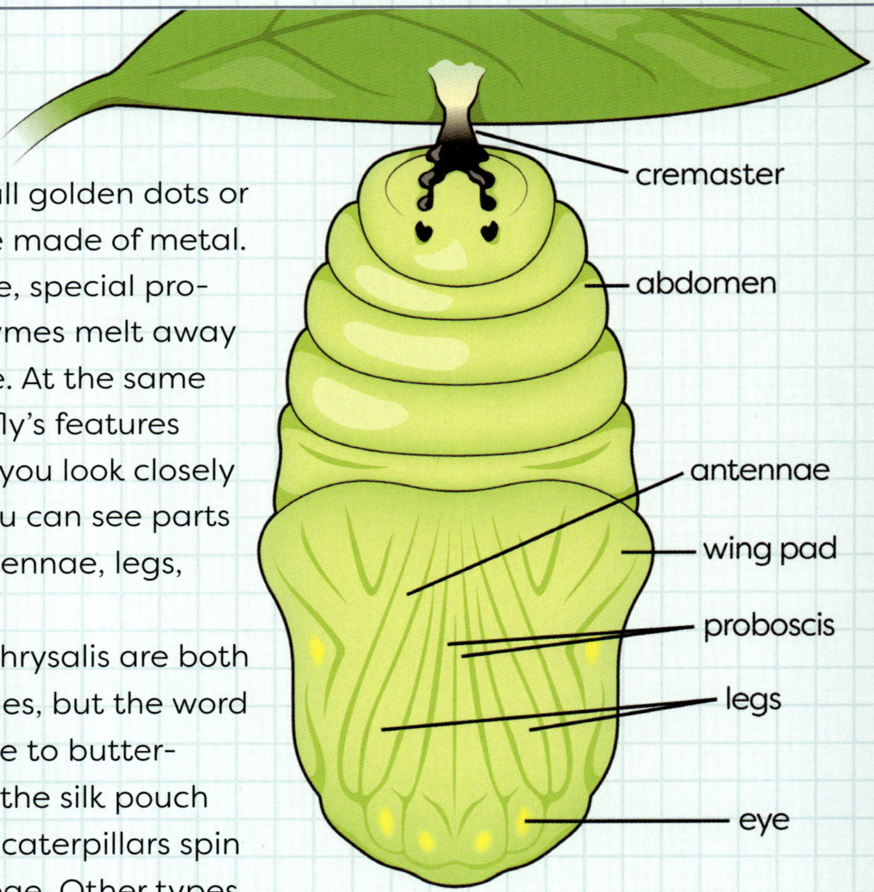

Becoming a Butterfly

Gradually, the chrysalis turns a dark color, and wing patterns begin to show. The adult butterfly splits open the chrysalis with its legs and pushes itself out of the casing. When it comes out, the butterfly is wet and has a round abdomen and shrunken wings. It looks nothing like a butterfly yet! The insect begins pumping liquid from its body into its crumpled wings to puff them up. It usually takes several hours for the wings to fully expand and dry. Once they have, the butterfly flies for the very first time. This is its maiden flight.

DID YOU KNOW?
The wings on butterflies are clear. The scales give them color. Some butterflies, like the glasswings from Central America, don't have scales and are see-through.

A CLOSER LOOK

Butterfly wings don't have muscles, so how do butterflies move? Since butterflies don't have bones, their muscles are attached to their exoskeletons. To fly, butterflies contract, or tighten, their thorax muscles. This motion pushes air under the wings and allows them to move through the air.

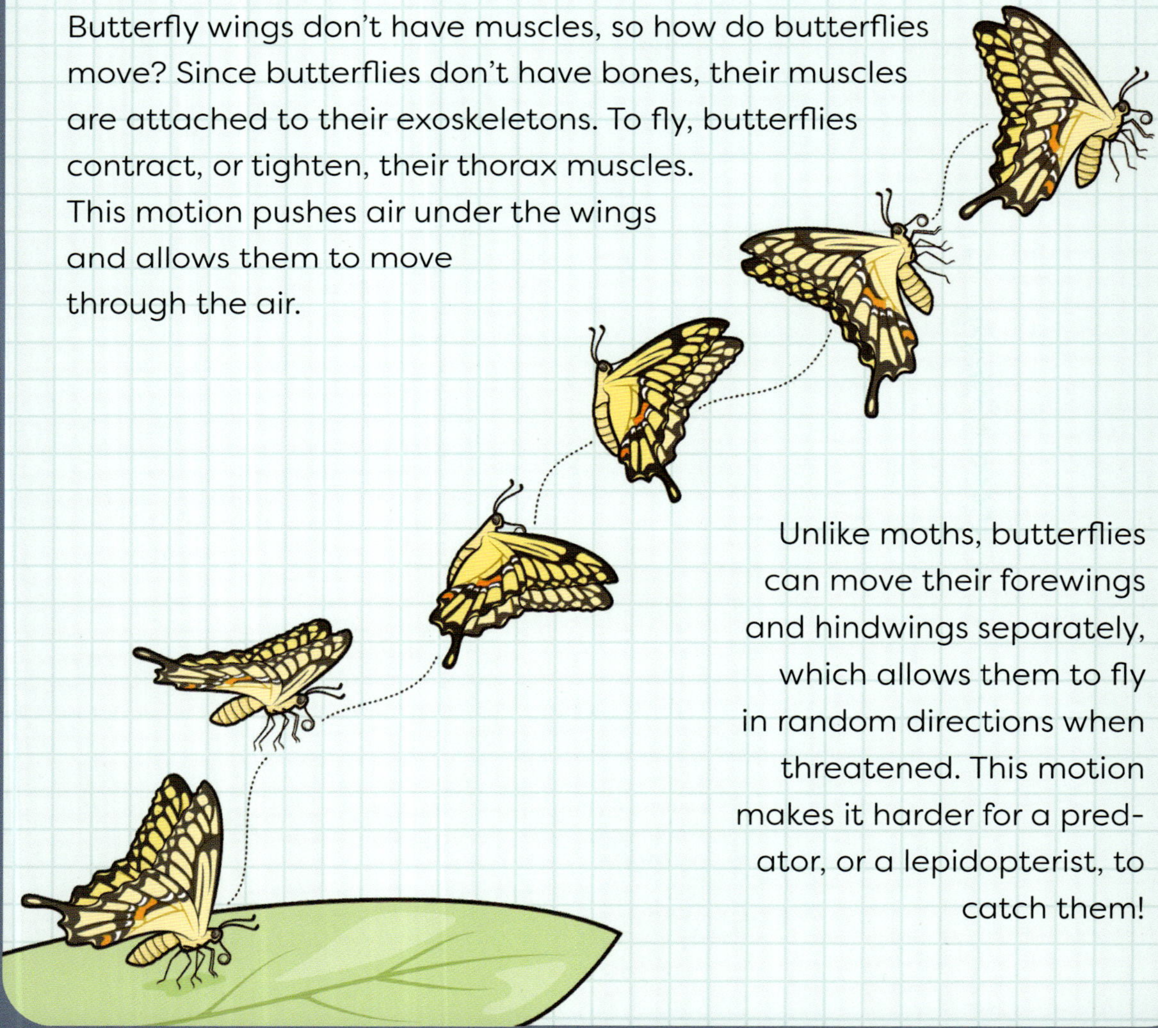

Unlike moths, butterflies can move their forewings and hindwings separately, which allows them to fly in random directions when threatened. This motion makes it harder for a predator, or a lepidopterist, to catch them!

Drinking Nectar

Butterflies need a lot of energy: to find a mate, migrate, and locate host plants. A butterfly's main source of fuel is nectar, a sugary liquid made by plants. But butterflies also feed on rotting fruits, tree sap, pollen, and even dead animals. Proboscises are basically coiled straws, so butterflies can only sip liquids. They must dissolve solids like pollen with their saliva before they can suck it up. Butterflies never eat solids, so they don't poop! They release only liquid waste.

Butterfly Behaviors

Butterflies have some unusual behaviors. They are cold-blooded and absorb heat from their environment, so you can think of them as solar-powered. On cold days, they sit in sunny spots with their wings wide open to soak up the sun's heat and warm their bodies. This process is called basking.

Puddling, or mud-puddling, is when butterflies suck up nutrients like salts and minerals from moist places such as mud. Many butterflies do this by themselves, but males of some species gather in large groups to drink. Butterflies also puddle on rotting animals or plants, animal poop, and even crocodile tears!

Butterflies rest at night. They may also rest during cold or rainy days. Although butterflies do not sleep like humans, they can become **dormant**. Most species do this alone on the undersides of leaves. Other species rest in large groups and return to the same spot each night. This behavior is called communal roosting, which scientists believe deters predators.

DID YOU KNOW?
The great orange-tip from Southeast Asia has a toxin very similar to the venom of the deadly cone snail.

Finding a Mate

The adult stage is often the shortest period of a butterfly's life cycle. Most adult butterflies live for only weeks. After emerging from the chrysalis, butterflies must find mates quickly. Mating is often seasonal. This timing ensures the caterpillars have plenty of food to eat when they hatch.

Many male butterflies find females using their wing patterns. The male gets close and signals the female using pheromones. Pheromones are a type of chemical message that others of the same species understand. If the female accepts his proposal, they mate.

DID YOU KNOW?
Butterflies can fight each other. They often tear each other's wings over territory or a chance at mating with a female.

A CLOSER LOOK

Caterpillars and butterflies are delicate, so how do they stay safe? Some caterpillars and butterflies use camouflage to blend in with their surroundings. Many look like twigs, leaves, and even bird poop. Others have eyespots to mimic, or copy, how other dangerous animals look.

Brightly colored species often taste bad or are poisonous. Their bodies store toxins from the host plants they eat. Their flashy colors are a warning sign to other animals to stay away. If a predator eats one, they will likely never try another. Some nonpoisonous butterflies mimic the same bright colors to avoid being eaten themselves.

Some caterpillars hire bodyguards. The pale blue butterfly oozes a sweet liquid called honeydew to attract ants. When the ants collect the honeydew, they take care of the caterpillars and protect them from predators.

Butterflies and the Environment

Our **ecosystems** depend on butterflies. Like bees, butterflies help with **pollination**, which is important to the life cycle of plants. In fact, some plants can only be pollinated by butterflies! Some plants grow too big and damage their habitat. Caterpillars eat these plants and keep them under control. Butterflies, in all stages, are also a main food source for many species. Butterflies are very sensitive to the environment. Any changes in their behaviors and numbers can help scientists spot problems in their ecosystem.

Unfortunately, butterflies are disappearing because of climate change, habitat loss, and the use of poisons. Many species are **endangered**, and some are now **extinct**. People are destroying butterfly habitats to create farmland and to build. The chemicals humans use to control weeds and insect pests harm butterflies and destroy their food sources.

Thankfully, people and organizations around the world are working to save endangered butterflies. How? By creating and protecting natural habitats and putting together programs that help increase butterfly numbers. As more people get involved, the future of butterflies gets brighter. It's so important for readers like you to get involved and take action!

PART TWO

BUTTERFLIES UP CLOSE

Have you ever spotted a butterfly in your backyard and wondered what it was called? In this section, you'll be introduced to 32 butterfly species you can find throughout most of the United States and southern Canada. Some of these species are found in other parts of the world, too. We've only provided the range of those butterflies in the United States and Canada so you know which species are common where you live. You will learn about where to locate them, what they eat, and how to identify them. How many will you find?

Silver-Spotted Skipper

Epargyreus clarus

SAY IT! *eh-par-jy-REE-us CLAR-us*

Skippers get their name from the way they quickly flutter and skip from plant to plant. The silver-spotted skipper is one of the largest skippers in North America. The large white spot on the underside of each wing flashes in the sun when the skipper flies. When feeding, these butterflies like to visit pink, purple, red, blue, or white flowers. They almost never sip from yellow ones. Female silver-spotted skippers sometimes lay their eggs on nearby plants instead of host plants. When the caterpillars hatch, they must crawl around to search for their food!

BUTTERFLY STATS

WHERE TO SPOT THEM: Most of the US and southernmost Canada

HABITAT: Brushy areas, river floodplains, prairie waterways, and swamps

WINGSPAN: 1.8 to 2.4 inches

HOST PLANTS: Legumes like black locust, false indigo, and butterfly pea

ADULT FOOD: Nectar from nonyellow flowers such as thistles, milkweed, and buttonbush

WHEN TO SPOT THEM: Northern areas: May–September; Southern areas: February–December

Sachem

Atalopedes campestris

SAY IT! *a-tal-o-PEE-dees CAMP-est-ris*

These little skippers look like tiny fighter jets when they are resting. This is because they hold their wings slightly open with their forewings at a different angle than their hindwings. You can recognize them by their quick, darting flight pattern. It would be difficult to find a sachem caterpillar, though. The tiny larva makes a kind of nest by using silk to attach leaves or grasses together. This gives it excellent protection from predators. It stays in the nest until it's time to feed—or poop!

BUTTERFLY STATS

WHERE TO SPOT THEM: Most of the US (except Rocky Mountains) and southernmost Canada

HABITAT: Open areas like lawns, fields, parks, and roadsides

WINGSPAN: 1.3 to 1.6 inches

HOST PLANTS: Grasses like St. Augustine, Bermuda, hairy crabgrass, and goosegrass

ADULT FOOD: Nectar from milkweed, marigold, asters, and buttonbush

WHEN TO SPOT THEM: Northern areas: May–November; Southern areas: March–December

Sootywing

Pholisora catullus

SAY IT! *FALL-ih-sor-ah CAT-ull-is*

Soot is the black dirt left when something burns. Can you see why this butterfly is called a sootywing? You'll find it in human-made habitats like landfills, parking lots, and even roadsides—which led to its nickname, the roadside rambler. The common sootywing was one of the first butterflies named in the Americas in the 1700s. Both males and females have little white spots on their wings, but the females have more. Common sootywings flutter in a zigzag pattern close the ground.

BUTTERFLY STATS

WHERE TO SPOT THEM: Most of the US, southern Quebec, and British Columbia

HABITAT: Open areas such as fields, parks, gardens, and roadsides

WINGSPAN: 1 to 1.3 inches

HOST PLANTS: Amaranths

ADULT FOOD: Nectar from flowers including dogbane, oxalis, milkweed, and melon

WHEN TO SPOT THEM: Northern areas: May–August; Southern areas: March–November

Checkered-Skipper

Pyrgus communis

SAY IT! *PEER-gus COM-you-nis*

Fuzzy and beautifully patterned, the common checkered-skipper has wings that look a little like a brown-and-white checkerboard. Male common checkered-skippers have bluish bodies and often patrol for mates in shady spots. Females usually have darker colors compared with males. To find these skippers, look for open, sunny places like meadows, landfills, pastures, and trails in the woods. You might confuse this species with the paler white checkered-skipper. The two species are so alike we can only tell them apart by dissecting them!

BUTTERFLY STATS

WHERE TO SPOT THEM: Most of the US, southern Canada, and Mexico

HABITAT: Open areas such as gardens, fields, roadsides, riverbanks, and parks

WINGSPAN: 0.8 to 1.5 inches

HOST PLANTS: Hollyhocks, poppy mallows, and globemallows

ADULT FOOD: Nectar from white flowers like fleabane and asters

WHEN TO SPOT THEM: Northern areas: March–September; Southern areas: year-round

TRACKING BUTTERFLIES

Did you know you can help butterfly scientists right now? There are many science programs you can join. Check out the North American Butterfly Monitoring Network or a local one in your state or county.

If you want to work with monarchs, Monarch Watch tags monarchs to help scientists study their migration. You can build a monarch waystation and register it with the organization. A monarch waystation is a garden habitat full of the monarch's favorite flowers and host plants. You can also report monarchs you find to organizations like Journey North. It uses your information to update monarch migration maps.

Phone apps, such as iNaturalist, are an easy way to share information about butterflies—or any other plants or creatures you find. Simply take a photo and post it to the app. This tool is also great for identifying butterflies if you're not sure what they are. You can report butterfly sightings to other online sites, such as the North American Butterfly Association (NABA), Butterflies and Moths of North America (BAMONA), and ebutterfly.

Pipevine Swallowtail

Battus philenor

SAY IT! *BAT-tus FIL-en-or*

Pipevine swallowtails are named after pipevine, their toxic host plant. The caterpillars eat the plant, which makes their bodies bitter-tasting and poisonous. The toxins stay in the insect's body, so the adult is a nasty mouthful, too. Other butterflies, like female eastern tiger swallowtails, mimic the pipevine swallowtails so predators think they are toxic, too. Some millipede species even mimic pipevine caterpillars! This species looks a lot like the spicebush swallowtail. How can you tell the difference? Pipevine swallowtails have one row of orange spots underneath their wings, and spicebush swallowtails have two rows.

BUTTERFLY STATS

WHERE TO SPOT THEM: Southern half of the US and New England, rarely into Canada

HABITAT: Open woodlands and fields

WINGSPAN: 2.8 to 5 inches

HOST PLANT: Pipevine

ADULT FOOD: Nectar from flowers including lantana, thistles, phlox, and ironweed

WHEN TO SPOT THEM: Northern areas: May–September; Southern areas: February–October

Giant Swallowtail

Papilio cresphontes

SAY IT! *pa-PIL-ee-oh CRES-fon-tees*

Also called an orange dog, the giant swallowtail is North America's largest butterfly. Its wingspan could cover a person's hand! Giant swallowtail caterpillars look like bird droppings, which means most predators leave them alone. Let's face it: Not many creatures want to eat poop! These butterflies are citrus farm pests. The caterpillars can take most or all the leaves off younger orange trees, which makes them unable to grow fruit.

BUTTERFLY STATS

WHERE TO SPOT THEM: Most of the eastern US, rarely into Canada

HABITAT: Woodlands and citrus groves

WINGSPAN: 5 to 6.8 inches

HOST PLANTS: Citrus trees, rue, hoptree, and prickly ash

ADULT FOOD: Nectar from flowers including lantana, goldenrod, milkweed, and honeysuckle

WHEN TO SPOT THEM: Northern areas: May–September; Southern areas: February–December; Deep South: year-round

Eastern Tiger Swallowtail

Papilio glaucus

SAY IT! *pa-PIL-ee-oh GLAW-kus*

Unlike most caterpillars, the larvae of this large species eat many different plants—more than any other swallowtail species in the world! Although most butterflies puddle on damp gravel or mud, this species also puddles on animal poop, rotting meat, and even animal pee. Eastern tiger swallowtail caterpillars in later instars are green and have large black and yellow spots that look like eyes behind their heads.

BUTTERFLY STATS

WHERE TO SPOT THEM: Eastern US and southern Ontario

HABITAT: Forest edges, roadsides, parks, open woods, riverbanks, creek-banks, and backyard gardens

WINGSPAN: 3 to 5.5 inches

HOST PLANTS: Bay laurel, tulip tree, ash, cottonwood, willow, birch, and others

ADULT FOOD: Nectar from flowers including asters, milkweed, wild cherry, and lilac

WHEN TO SPOT THEM: Northern areas: May–September; Southern areas: February–November

Black Swallowtail

Papilio polyxenes

SAY IT! *pa-PIL-ee-oh PAUL-ix-ee-nees*

When it comes to mating, male black swallowtails do their best to impress females. They have a rare behavior called lekking, or lek mating. This is when a large group of males gathers to attract visiting females. Males at the lekking site need to compete with other males for a spot, so a female knows whichever male she picks will make a good mate. Black swallowtail caterpillars' host plants are common herbs, so you can often find them in backyard gardens.

BUTTERFLY STATS

WHERE TO SPOT THEM: Most common east of Rocky Mountains and southern Canada

HABITAT: Open areas like fields or meadows

WINGSPAN: 3.5 to 4.5 inches

HOST PLANTS: Herbs like dill, parsley, rue, and fennel

ADULT FOOD: Nectar from flowers including thistles, lantana, red clover, and milkweed

WHEN TO SPOT THEM: Northern areas: April–October; Southern areas: February–November

Zebra Swallowtail

Protographium marcellus

SAY IT! *pro-to-GRAF-ee-um mar-SEL-us*

Can you guess why this butterfly is called a zebra swallowtail? With their black-and-white stripes and long tails, zebra swallowtails are one of the most unique-looking butterflies in North America. When it's time to lay her eggs, the female looks for a good host plant. Young plants with soft juicy leaves are best for her young. She lays her eggs one at a time on the leaves or trunks of a pawpaw tree. The newly hatched caterpillars will eat one another, so she must keep the eggs separated!

BUTTERFLY STATS

WHERE TO SPOT THEM: Eastern US and southernmost Canada

HABITAT: Damp areas near woodlands and grasslands

WINGSPAN: 2.5 to 4 inches

HOST PLANT: Pawpaw tree

ADULT FOOD: Nectar from flowers like lilac, redbud, verbena, milkweed, and rotting fruit

WHEN TO SPOT THEM: Northern areas: April–August; Southern areas: March–December

GROWING A BUTTERFLY

Butterfly kits are used to learn how butterflies grow. When using a kit, here are some things to keep in mind to avoid harming the caterpillars or the environment.

1. Keep the pop-up house that comes with your kit. It is a great place to keep and observe wild butterflies. Place a paper plate in the bottom to help keep it clean.
2. The caterpillar food that came with your kit is made for that species. Make sure you're feeding correctly; for example, do not give monarch caterpillars food that was made for painted ladies.
3. Most kits come with a voucher you can use to get live larvae. Check the weather in your area before ordering them. Extreme cold and heat can kill the caterpillars.
4. If a caterpillar falls during pupation in its container, leave it until it hardens. Once it hardens, you can move the chrysalis to the floor of the mesh cage. Butterflies usually figure out how to climb up when they emerge!

5. Do not release butterflies into the wild unless the kit says you can. Double-check that the species you are growing lives in your area. If it does, release the butterflies soon after they can fly. Otherwise, you'll end up with lots of hungry baby caterpillars!

6. If you find out that you cannot release your butterflies, please reach out to your local university, nature center, or museum to get tips on what to do.

Sleepy Orange

Eurema nicippe

SAY IT! *YOUR-ee-mah ni-SIP-ee*

Sleepy orange butterflies are anything but sleepy! When disturbed, these little creatures are very energetic as they quickly dart and flutter away. Sleepy oranges get their name from a spot on their front wings that looks like a tiny closed eye. These butterflies gather in groups of 20 or more to puddle on wet mud or sand. Males and females look mostly the same, but males are often smaller and brighter in color than the females. Sleepy oranges that live in the north migrate south for the winter and lay eggs the following spring.

BUTTERFLY STATS

WHERE TO SPOT THEM: Most of the southern half of the US, rarely into southern Canada

HABITAT: Open areas like fields or meadows

WINGSPAN: 1.5 to 2.3 inches

HOST PLANTS: Pea plants

ADULT FOOD: Nectar from a variety of flowers

WHEN TO SPOT THEM: Northern areas: July–September; Southern areas: February–December

Cloudless Sulphur

Phoebis sennae

SAY IT! *FEE-bus sin-NAY*

No matter where you live in the United States, you've probably seen these cheerful little common butterflies. The caterpillars of this species are great at camouflage. Their bodies are green during the time they feed on green leaves and then turn yellow when they start feeding on yellow flowers. Adults tend to rest on yellow flowers because they blend in perfectly. When it's dark or cloudy, cloudless sulphurs rest on the undersides of leaves. This species is very attracted to red flowers and will sometimes flutter around other red objects, even car taillights.

BUTTERFLY STATS

WHERE TO SPOT THEM: Most of the US and southern Ontario

HABITAT: Open areas such as fields, roadsides, and even beaches

WINGSPAN: 2.5 to 3.2 inches

HOST PLANT: Pea plants

ADULT FOOD: Nectar from flowers with long tubes such as hibiscus, lantana, and morning glory

WHEN TO SPOT THEM: Northern areas: July–September; Southern areas: February–November

Southern Dogface

Zerene cesonia

SAY IT! *ze-REEN-ee ces-OWN-ee-uh*

The southern dogface might just be the easiest butterfly to identify. If you look closely at the top of their front wings, you can see a pattern that looks like a yellow poodle's face. This is how they got their name. Like the cloudless sulphur and sleepy orange, the southern dogface migrates south and overwinters as an adult. These butterflies change their colors with the seasons. During the summer they are mostly yellow underneath. In fall, they are tinted pink.

BUTTERFLY STATS

WHERE TO SPOT THEM: Mostly in the southernmost US but can be found in most of the country

HABITAT: Open areas such as fields, road edges, and open woodlands

WINGSPAN: 2.3 to 3 inches

HOST PLANTS: Small-leaved plants in the pea family, including alfalfa, clover, and indigo

ADULT FOOD: Nectar from flowers including verbena, tickseed, and bluet

WHEN TO SPOT THEM: Northern areas: May–September; Southern areas: year-round

Cabbage White

Pieris rapae

SAY IT! *PEE-er-is RAP-ee*

Many people confuse these little butterflies with moths because they look so plain. The cabbage white is also known as the imported cabbageworm. Years ago, it probably lived only in Europe. As people started trading goods by ships, the cabbage white hitched rides aboard and spread across the world. Cabbage whites are pests because they eat crops like kale, cabbage, broccoli, and bok choy. Males have one black spot on the top of their wings, and females have two.

BUTTERFLY STATS

WHERE TO SPOT THEM: Most of the US and southern Canada

HABITAT: Open areas such as gardens, roadsides, fields, and lawns

WINGSPAN: 1.3 to 1.8 inches

HOST PLANTS: Brussels sprouts, cabbage, broccoli, bok choy, and cauliflower

ADULT FOOD: Nectar from a wide variety of flowering plants

WHEN TO SPOT THEM: Northern areas: March–September; Southern areas: February–December; Deep South: year-round

Checkered White

Pontia protodice

SAY IT! *PON-tee-uh PRO-toe-dee-see*

Checkered whites, also known as southern cabbage worms, are also considered pests, although they don't cause as much damage as cabbage whites. Although they do eat crops, checkered whites prefer to munch on common roadside weeds like Virginia peppergrass and prairie pepperweed. Whereas most caterpillars like to feast on the leaves of their host plant, checkered white caterpillars prefer to munch on flowers and buds.

BUTTERFLY STATS

WHERE TO SPOT THEM: Mostly southernmost US but can be found in most of the US and rarely southern Canada

HABITAT: Open areas such as deserts, plains, and grasslands

WINGSPAN: 1.3 to 1.8 inches

HOST PLANTS: Mustard plants, Virginia pepperweed, peppergrass, sometimes cabbage and broccoli

ADULT FOOD: Nectar from a wide variety of flowering plants

WHEN TO SPOT THEM: Northern areas: May–September; Southern areas: March–November

Hackberry Emperor

Asterocampa celtis

SAY IT! *AS-ter-oh-camp-uh SELL-tees*

Not all butterflies like to sip nectar from flowers. The hackberry emperor would rather eat tree sap, rotting fruit, or the liquids from carrion (dead animals) or dung (animal poop). They also seem to like the salt in sweat, so don't be surprised if this butterfly lands on your skin to take a drink. During the winter, hackberry emperor caterpillars hibernate in groups, safely rolled up in fallen hackberry leaves on the forest floor. Once spring comes, the larvae come out of their leaf sleeping bags and climb up the tree to feed again. They sometimes eat all the leaves off an entire tree!

BUTTERFLY STATS

WHERE TO SPOT THEM: Eastern US and southeastern Canada

HABITAT: Moist, shaded areas such as river edges, wooded roadsides, and wooded streams

WINGSPAN: 1.5 to 2.5 inches

HOST PLANT: Hackberry trees

ADULT FOOD: Rotting fruit, sap, dung, and carrion

WHEN TO SPOT THEM: May–October

Monarch

Danaus plexippus

SAY IT! *dan-AY-us PLEK-see-puss*

Most people know what a monarch looks like. These butterflies are one of the most recognized in North America. They are known for their incredible migration from Canada to Mexico, but you can find monarchs all over the world. They live in South America, New Zealand, Australia, the Philippines, and even Northern Africa. In 2009, monarch butterflies went to space! Astronauts raised them on the International Space Station. Poisonous milkweed is the caterpillar's only food. The bright orange color of the adult's wings is a clear warning for predators to leave it alone.

BUTTERFLY STATS

WHERE TO SPOT THEM: Most of the US and southern Canada

HABITAT: Open areas like fields or meadows

WINGSPAN: 3.5 to 4 inches

HOST PLANT: Milkweed

ADULT FOOD: Nectar of various flowers, including milkweed

WHEN TO SPOT THEM: Northern areas: May–September; Southern areas: February–December

A CLOSER LOOK

Monarchs are famous for their North American migration. But did you know it takes more than one **generation** of monarch butterflies to complete the trip there and back?

In the spring, monarchs lay eggs in the southern United States. When those caterpillars become butterflies, they begin flying north. It usually takes three or four generations of monarchs to make it up to the northern states and southern Canada.

Once the weather starts becoming colder in the north, a special group of monarchs gets ready for their flight. They are called the super generation. These special monarchs fly up to 3,000 miles south to join other monarch migrants. These groups gather at the same small overwintering sites in Mexico every year. Once the weather begins to warm up, the super generation flies back north to the southern United States, mates, and lays eggs. Then the entire cycle begins again!

Gulf Fritillary

Agraulis vanillae

SAY IT! *AH-gro-lis VA-nil-ee*

Like the monarch, the gulf fritillary is bright orange to warn predators to back off. If a bird or another predator doesn't get the message, this butterfly has a second defense. It releases a super stinky liquid from its abdomen that predators find disgusting. The caterpillars feast on passion vines, a poisonous plant with large unique flowers. Females lay their eggs on most parts of this host plant, including leaves, stems, and tendrils.

BUTTERFLY STATS

WHERE TO SPOT THEM: Southern US, some in the central US, rarely as far north as North Dakota

HABITAT: Fields, meadows, woodland edges

WINGSPAN: 2.5 to 3.8 inches

HOST PLANTS: Passion vines

ADULT FOOD: Nectar from flowers including lantana, pentas, and shepherd's needle

WHEN TO SPOT THEM: Northern areas: January–November; Southern areas: year-round

Great Spangled Fritillary

Speyeria cybele

SAY IT! *SPAY-er-ee-ah sib-EL-ee*

Great spangled fritillaries are the most common fritillary in the eastern United States, so you likely have seen one. Many butterfly species have multiple generation cycles a year, but this species has only one. After mating in the summer, the females lay their eggs near violets, their host plants. Once the caterpillars hatch, they overwinter until spring. When spring comes, they hide under leaves during the day and feed at night. The larvae molt six times before pupating—more than many other butterflies!

BUTTERFLY STATS

WHERE TO SPOT THEM: Most of the US (except southwestern states) and southern Canada

HABITAT: Open moist areas including fields, meadows, and woodlands

WINGSPAN: 2.5 to 4 inches

HOST PLANT: Violets

ADULT FOOD: Nectar from flowers including thistles, milkweed, butterfly bush, and purple coneflower

WHEN TO SPOT THEM: June–September

American Snout

Libytheana carinenta

SAY IT! *lih-BITH-ee-ay-nah CAR-een-ent-ah*

Look at the shape of this butterfly's head. The American snout appears to have a long nose, or snout. But that is not a nose—it's the butterfly's long mouth-parts! This butterfly hangs upside down on branches and twigs, imitating dead leaves for camouflage. American snouts are known for their huge migrations in Texas and Mexico. In 1921, a huge swarm flew across a 250-mile-wide area in Texas. Scientists believe more than 6 billion butterflies were spotted. There are fewer than 15 known species of snout butterfly in the world. The American snout is the only one you might see regularly north of Mexico.

BUTTERFLY STATS

WHERE TO SPOT THEM: Most of the US and southern Canada

HABITAT: Brushy fields, roadsides, and forest edges

WINGSPAN: 1.5 to 2 inches

HOST PLANT: Hackberry

ADULT FOOD: Prefers white and yellow flowers such as asters, dogbane, and goldenrod

WHEN TO SPOT THEM: May–August

Viceroy

Limenitis archippus

SAY IT! *li-men-EYE-tiss AR-ki-pus*

This isn't a monarch butterfly. It's a viceroy! Viceroys are well-known monarch mimics. By looking like poisonous monarchs, they scare away predators who know monarchs taste bad. But some scientists now think viceroys taste bad to predators, too! This means viceroys and monarchs might be mimicking each other, which makes their warnings to predators extra effective. If you are wondering whether you found a viceroy or monarch, look for the viceroy's black band on its back wings.

BUTTERFLY STATS

WHERE TO SPOT THEM: Most of the US and southern Canada

HABITAT: Open areas like fields or meadows

WINGSPAN: 2.5 to 3.5 inches

HOST PLANTS: Willows, poplars, and cottonwoods

ADULT FOOD: Nectar from flowers including aster, goldenrod, and thistles; also decaying fungi, dung, carrion, and aphid honeydew when flowers are unavailable

WHEN TO SPOT THEM: Northern areas: May–September; Southern areas: February–December; Deep South: year-round

Common Buckeye

Junonia coenia

SAY IT! *JOO-no-nee-ah SIN-ee-ah*

If you see a small butterfly with what look like bullseyes on its wings, you've found a common buckeye. This species gets its name from the target-shaped eyespots on its wings. These spots do a great job at scaring predators into thinking they are looking at a larger animal. The caterpillars of this species have spiny bodies that keep most lizards and birds away. This butterfly's proboscis is quite short, so it prefers flowers with easy-to-reach nectar.

BUTTERFLY STATS

WHERE TO SPOT THEM: Southern US with migrants farther north and into southern Canada

HABITAT: Open, sunny areas like fields, pastures, gardens, roadsides, and weed lots

WINGSPAN: 2 to 2.5 inches

HOST PLANTS: Toadflax, snapdragons, plantains, and wild petunias

ADULT FOOD: Nectars from flowers including asters, dogbane, chicory, and tickseed flower

WHEN TO SPOT THEM: Northern areas: May–October; Southern areas: year-round

A CLOSER LOOK

Adult butterflies usually have short lives. Although their entire life cycle can take several months, most species live as adults for only two to four weeks. Many species can live much longer. For example, the scarce green-striped white from Africa can live up to 15 years as an adult!

The purpose of an adult butterfly is to mate and lay eggs. Once the eggs are laid, most butterfly moms don't stick around to care for their babies. Depending on where they live, many butterfly species produce several batches of eggs in a year. That's why you might see a particular species fluttering about for several months at a time.

Eastern dappled white, a relative of the scarce green-striped white

Mourning Cloak

Nymphalis antiopa

SAY IT! *NIM-fal-is an-tee-OH-pa*

Mourning cloaks have long lives—for butterflies. They have an adult lifespan of up to 11 to 12 months, making them one of the longest-living butterflies species in the world! Although native to North America, this butterfly also lives in northern South America, Europe, and Central Asia. These butterflies are also easy to spot because they don't look like any others in North America. Mourning cloak butterflies spend the winter tucked under tree bark for protection. Sometimes you can see them fluttering about while there is still spring snow on the ground.

BUTTERFLY STATS

WHERE TO SPOT THEM: All of North America south of the tundra

HABITAT: Anywhere their host plants are found

WINGSPAN: 2.5 to 4 inches

HOST PLANTS: Various trees, such as willows, elms, cottonwoods, birch trees, and hackberries

ADULT FOOD: Tree sap, especially from oaks; rotting fruit; sometimes flower nectar

WHEN TO SPOT THEM: Year-round

Pearl Crescent

Phyciodes tharos

SAY IT! *fye-SEE-oh-dees THAR-os*

Pearl crescents are feisty little butterflies. The males are quite **territorial** and will dart after other males that wander into their turf. Sometimes they will chase other insects, birds, or even Frisbees! Pearl crescents can also be curious about humans. Female pearl crescents lay eggs in groups called clutches. During early instars, the caterpillars stay in large groups to feed beneath a silk web. Gradually, they become more independent until they are feeding alone.

BUTTERFLY STATS

WHERE TO SPOT THEM: Most of the US (except Pacific Northwest) and southern Canada

HABITAT: Open areas such as pastures, field, meadows, and woods

WINGSPAN: 1.3 to 1.8 inches

HOST PLANTS: Asters

ADULT FOOD: Nectar from a variety of flowers like asters, milkweed, and thistles

WHEN TO SPOT THEM: Northern areas: April–November; Southern areas: year-round

Question Mark

Polygonia interrogationis

SAY IT! *po-lee-GOH-nee-uh in-ter-oh-gat-ee-OH-nis*

Can you guess why this butterfly is called a question mark? Look carefully! This species gets its name from the silvery marking on each hindwing, which looks like a question mark. Like the pearl crescent, males of this species defend their territories, so you might see them chasing other male butterflies or even birds. The eastern comma butterfly also sports a punctuation mark on its wing. Be careful not to confuse the two!

BUTTERFLY STATS

WHERE TO SPOT THEM: Eastern US and southern Canada

HABITAT: Open wooded areas

WINGSPAN: 2 to 3 inches

HOST PLANTS: Elms, hackberry, Japanese hop, nettles, and false nettle

ADULT FOOD: Rotting fruit, tree sap, dung, and carrion; rarely flower nectar

WHEN TO SPOT THEM: Northern areas: May–September; Southern areas: March–October

Red Admiral

Vanessa atalanta

SAY IT! *va-NESS-uh a-ta-LAN-tah*

Red admiral females are very picky when it comes to finding mates. They mate only with males that have a territory. The red admirals' territories have oval shapes. Males protect their territories by constantly patrolling, or flying around them—up to 30 times an hour. Females choose only the strongest males for mates, so males take their job very seriously. These butterflies are not afraid of people and sometimes even use humans as perches.

BUTTERFLY STATS

WHERE TO SPOT THEM: Most of the US and southern Canada

HABITAT: Moist wooded areas, marshes, and parks

WINGSPAN: 1.8 to 2.5 inches

HOST PLANTS: Nettles

ADULT FOOD: Tree sap, rotting fruit, bird droppings; rarely nectar

WHEN TO SPOT THEM: Northern areas: March–October; Southern areas: year-round

Painted Lady

Vanessa cardui

SAY IT! *va-NESS-uh CAR-dew-eye*

People all around the world love painted lady butterflies. They live on every continent except South America and Antarctica. Much like monarchs, painted ladies migrate in colder seasons. During migration, these butterflies can fly 100 miles or more in a single day. Some swarms are so large they can be picked up by weather radar equipment. One weather station discovered a cloud of painted ladies flying over Colorado that was 70 miles wide. That's as wide as New Hampshire!

BUTTERFLY STATS

WHERE TO SPOT THEM: Most of the US and southern Canada

HABITAT: Almost everywhere, especially open areas

WINGSPAN: 1.5 to 2.7 inches

HOST PLANTS: A variety of plants, including thistles, mallows, and legumes

ADULT FOOD: Nectar from flowers including thistles, asters, cosmos, buttonbush, and milkweeds

WHEN TO SPOT THEM: Northern areas: May–October; Southern areas: year-round

BUTTERFLY GARDENING

Sometimes you don't even have to leave your own backyard to find butterflies. If you provide the right plants, butterflies will find you!

Pick a Spot: Pick an area in your garden (or choose a container) to grow your plants. Consider how much sunlight, water, and space plants will need to grow properly.

Check Your Zone: Many plants only grow well in certain climates. Make sure you are planting for your hardiness zone, which can be found online.

Choose a Plant: Research what butterflies are in your area and what nectar plants they like. Don't forget to consider host plants for the caterpillars, too! You can find this information online and at local garden centers. Make sure they'll do well in the spot or container you've chosen.

Avoid Pesticides: When buying any nectar or host plants, make sure they are pesticide-free.

Once the butterflies find your plants, they will probably return often. Keep a journal or list of all the butterflies that visit.

JUNIOR SCIENTISTS IN ACTION

Harvester

Feniseca tarquinius

SAY IT! *FEN-i-seck-uh TAR-kin-ee-us*

Meet North America's only true **carnivorous** butterfly, the harvester! Harvester caterpillars feed on woolly aphids, which are a type of insect. After mating, female harvesters lay their eggs near colonies of woolly aphids or other host insects. When the caterpillars hatch, they eat the aphids. Young caterpillars may trap the aphids with silk because they are not strong enough to hold the aphids while they feed. To protect themselves from ants, harvester larvae make a protective suit of armor using dead aphids or their old skins attached with silk.

BUTTERFLY STATS

WHERE TO SPOT THEM: Eastern half of the US and southern Canada

HABITAT: Mixed woodlands, especially near water sources

WINGSPAN: 1 to 1.3 inches

HOST INSECTS: Woolly aphids and sometimes scale insects and treehoppers

ADULT FOOD: Aphid honeydew, dung, carrion, and damp sand

WHEN TO SPOT THEM: Northern areas: May–August; Southern areas: February–September

American Copper

Lycaena phlaeas

SAY IT! *ly-SEE-nuh FLEE-us*

It may be tiny, but the American copper is an aggressive species. Males will chase almost anything that moves through their territories. Even a flying bird's shadow is enough to make a male take notice. After mating, females lay their eggs on top of their host plant leaves. After they hatch, the caterpillars move to the underside. There, they feast on the leaves without chewing all the way through. This makes window-like patterns in the leaves. American copper pupae don't hang like most butterflies. Instead, they lie in the leaves, twigs, and other plant matter on the ground.

BUTTERFLY STATS

WHERE TO SPOT THEM: Throughout the US (except southern states) and southern Canada

HABITAT: Rocky areas in northern range, open areas in southern range

WINGSPAN: 1 to 1.2 inches

HOST PLANTS: Buckwheat

ADULT FOOD: Nectar from flowers including buttercups, yarrow, and daisies

WHEN TO SPOT THEM: Northern areas: June–September; Southern areas: April–September

Western Pygmy Blue

Brephidium exilis

SAY IT! *BRE-phid-ee-um EX-ih-lis*

You will have to look closely to see the western pygmy blue; it's about as large as your thumbnail! This butterfly is the smallest in North America and one of the smallest in the world. The western pygmy blue has a very special relationship with ants. Ants protect the larvae from predators. In return, the ants get to eat the sugary honeydew from the caterpillars. You can spot these butterflies on hot, sunny days, when they're most active.

BUTTERFLY STATS

WHERE TO SPOT THEM: Most common in the southwestern US

HABITAT: Salt marshes, desert areas, and prairies

WINGSPAN: 0.5 to 0.7 inch

HOST PLANTS: Goosefoot, saltbush, pigweed, saltwart, and sea purslane

ADULT FOOD: Nectar from flowers including lantana, goldenrod, and asters

WHEN TO SPOT THEM: Northern areas: July–September; Southern areas: year-round

Gray Hairstreak

Strymon melinus

SAY IT! *STRY-mon MEL-in-us*

Many butterflies lay their eggs on the leaves of their host plants, but gray hairstreaks lay them on the flowers. The newly hatched caterpillars eat both the flowers and any developing fruit. The gray hairstreak has a tricky way of dealing with predators. If approached, the butterfly rubs its closed back wings together. This movement makes the tails of its wings wiggle like a pair of antennae. Predators that take the bait may manage to grab a piece of wing, but that's better than the butterfly losing its head!

BUTTERFLY STATS

WHERE TO SPOT THEM: Most of the US and southern Canada

HABITAT: Almost anywhere, including open spaces, grassy areas, roadsides, and gardens

WINGSPAN: 1 to 1.4 inches

HOST PLANTS: A variety of plants, including pea and mallow

ADULT FOOD: Nectar from flowers including milkweed, goldenrod, and sweet clover

WHEN TO SPOT THEM: Northern areas: May–September; Southern areas: February–November

CREATE YOUR OWN JOURNAL

Thinking of being a lepidopterist? Start by creating your own butterfly observation journal! Use the journal to sketch butterflies you find, take notes on different behaviors, and keep a list of all the butterflies you've seen in different areas.

A composition or spiral notebook works great, but you can get as fancy as you'd like. There are journals made specifically for field notes, and some are even waterproof! Make your journal your own by decorating the cover. Keep a pen or pencil with your journal so you can quickly scribble notes or a sketch. Did you find part of a wing or a dead leaf of a host plant? Tape them on your pages for safekeeping!

When recording butterfly behaviors, pay attention to details like weather and time. For example, if you see a butterfly feeding, ask yourself these questions:

- What is it eating?
- Is it flapping its wings, holding them together, or spreading them out?
- Is it sunny or cloudy?
- Are you in a wooded or open area?

Pay attention to details of the butterfly such as colors, wing shape, and flight pattern in case you don't get a chance to snap a photo.

Mormon Metalmark

Apodemia mormo

SAY IT! *ap-o-DEM-ee-uh MOR-mo*

Mormon metalmarks are lively little butterflies that live in dry areas. They tend to hang out in bright, sunny areas and flutter energetically low to the ground. The caterpillars hatch from small clutches of pinkish-white eggs laid on the undersides of leaves. These larvae hide in shelters they make out of leaves and silk during the day and come out to feed at night.

BUTTERFLY STATS

WHERE TO SPOT THEM: Western US and southwestern Canada

HABITAT: Dry fields, dry rocky valleys, and semidesert areas

WINGSPAN: 0.9 to 1.3 inches

HOST PLANT: Buckwheat

ADULT FOOD: Nectar from flowers including buckwheat and yellow flowers such as ragwort

WHEN TO SPOT THEM: Northern areas: July–September; Southern areas: March–October

Northern Metalmark

Calephelis borealis

SAY IT! *CAL-eh-fel-is BORE-ee-al-is*

If you are able to spot a northern metalmark, you are lucky! This butterfly has become quite rare in the areas where it used to be found. Its habitat is slowly being destroyed, and its host plants are getting choked out by other plants. Often mistaken for a small moth, this species rests with its wings flat. When flying, the northern metalmark looks floppy and mothlike. If you want to look for one of these butterflies, check near rock outcrops like limestone, shale, slate, and phyllite.

BUTTERFLY STATS

WHERE TO SPOT THEM: Connecticut through Pennsylvania, Missouri, Arkansas, and Oklahoma

HABITAT: Rocky areas where host plants are found

WINGSPAN: 1.1 to 1.4 inches

HOST PLANT: Ragworts

ADULT FOOD: Nectar from flowers including yarrow, goldenrod, and daisies

WHEN TO SPOT THEM: June–July

BUTTERFLY LIFE LIST

Use this table to track your butterfly sightings. Life lists are a way to keep track of every species you come across. You can use this list to compare butterflies in your area to those in other places. Some people even use life lists to compete with friends or others in an organization or club!

SCIENTIFIC NAME	COMMON NAME	LIFE STAGE	LOCATION	DATE	TIME

BUTTERFLY LIFE LIST *CONTINUED*

SCIENTIFIC NAME	COMMON NAME	LIFE STAGE	LOCATION	DATE	TIME

MORE TO DISCOVER

Books

BUTTERFLIES (PETERSON FIELD GUIDES: FOR YOUNG NATURALISTS) **BY KAREN STRAY NOLTING AND JONATHAN LATIMER**

Learn how to identify common North American butterfly species with this field guide.

CATERPILLARS, BUGS AND BUTTERFLIES: TAKE-ALONG GUIDE **BY MEL BORING**

Packed with activities, fun facts, and tips for identifying butterflies and other insects.

HOW TO RAISE MONARCH BUTTERFLIES **BY CAROL PASTERNAK**

Learn how to raise a monarch from caterpillar to butterfly!

ULTIMATE BUGOPEDIA **BY DARLYNE MURAWSKI AND NANCY HONOVICH**

Learn oodles of interesting bug facts with this colorful book from National Geographic Kids.

Websites

BUGGUIDE.NET
Learn about North American insects with images, information, and tips on identification.

BUTTERFLIESANDMOTHS.ORG
Butterflies and Moths of North America (BAMONA) is an organization that collects and shares species information. You can even submit your own photographs of butterflies, moths, and caterpillars.

BUTTERFLY-FUN-FACTS.COM
Educational blog written by butterfly enthusiasts of Shady Oak Butterfly Farm.

MONARCHWATCH.ORG
Monarch Watch is a conservation and research program that focuses on monarch butterflies. You can submit your own tagging data to help scientists.

PLANTHARDINESS.ARS.USDA.GOV
Check your zip code in the Plant Hardiness Zone Map to learn which plants to grow in your butterfly garden.

GLOSSARY

ADAPTATION (A-DAHP-TAY-SHUN): A physical or behavioral change in a plant or animal that gives it a better chance of survival

CARNIVOROUS (KAR-NI-VORE-US): A type of animal (or plant) that feeds on animal meat or tissue

CHRYSALIS (KRIS-UH-LIS): The pupa stage of a butterfly; also the hard outer covering of a butterfly pupa

DORMANT (DOR-MUHNT): When a living thing's growth and activities are stopped for a period of time

ECOSYSTEM (EE-CO-SIS-TUM): A group of different living things that interact with each other and their surroundings

ENDANGERED (IN-DANE-JERD): At risk of going extinct if not protected

EVOLVE (EE-VOLV): To develop and change gradually over time

EXTINCT (EK-STINGKT): When a species is no longer in existence

GENERATION (GEN-UHR-AY-SHUN): A group living at the same time that are about the same age

HIBERNATE (HI-BUR-NATE): A sleeping or resting state during winter. Butterflies and other insects do not technically hibernate, but the term is often used to describe any animal resting through winter.

HOST PLANT: A specific plant or group of plants that a caterpillar feeds on

INSECT (IN-SEKT): A group of invertebrates with six legs, three main body parts, and antennae

INSTAR (IN-STAHR): The time between molts

INVERTEBRATE (IN-VER-TEH-BRAYT): An animal that does not have a backbone

LARVA (LAR-VUH): The form that hatches from an egg in species that go through complete metamorphosis

LEPIDOPTERIST (LEP-UH-DOP-TER-IHST): A scientist who specializes in butterflies and moths

METAMORPHOSIS (MET-AH-MOHR-FAH-SIS): The multistep process some insects go through to develop from an egg to an adult

MIGRATE (MY-GREAT): To travel from one place to another according to seasons

MOLT (MOHLT): To shed an old outer layer in order to grow

OVERWINTER (OWE-VER-WIN-TUR): To live throughout the winter

POLLINATION (PAH-LIH-NAY-SHUN): The transfer of pollen from one plant to another of the same species so new seeds can form

PUPA (PYOO-PUH): The stage between the larval stage and the adult stage of an insect that goes through complete metamorphosis

SPECIES (SPEE-SEEZ): A group of living things that has many characteristics in common and can mate to make others of their kind

TERRITORIAL (TERR-UH-TOR-EE-ULL): When an insect or animal keeps a territory (area) of its own and fights to defend it

WINGSPAN: The measurement of the longest distance across both forewings, tip to tip

INDEX

ABOUT THE AUTHOR

Lauren Davidson is a practicing entomologist whose career has primarily focused on butterflies and moths. Considered a lepidopterist, Lauren spends her work life caring for and studying butterflies from all around the world. This interest in butterflies and other insects started at a young age while routinely visiting the Cockrell Butterfly Center at the Houston Museum of Natural Science. Today, this passion continues as she manages the very place that inspired her. Visit her on Instagram @bugsologist.